A Musical Celebration

CHRISTMAS, SING NOEL!

Created and
Arranged by
Ed Kee

Orchestrated by
Russell Mauldin

Also available:

Listening Cassette	C-5469N
Preview Pak	C/BK-5469
Stereo/Split-Track Accompaniment Cassette	TR/S-3197C
Stereo/Split-Track Accompaniment CD	TR/S-3197CD
Orchestration	OR-3197
Conductor's Score	CS-3197
Rehearsal Tracks	RT-5469
Bulletins (pak of 100)	BU-3197
Posters (pak of 12)	P-3197

Instrumentation:
Flute 1,2
Oboe 1
Horn 1
Trumpet 1,2,3
Trombone 1,2,3
Percussion 1,2
Harp
Violin 1,2
Viola 1
Cello 1,2
Bass 1
Rhythm (Piano, Synth, Bass, Drums)

Performance Time: 40 Minutes

BRENTWOOD
MUSIC

Contents

The Accompaniment Cassette and Compact Disc provide two complete accompaniment options:
1. Split Trax (Left Channel - Instruments, Right Channel - Vocals) and
2. Instruments Only.
The Compact Disc option is indicated by two numbers. For example, **1•70** means that the Stereo Accompaniment for "Christmas, Sing Noel!" begins at point 1, while the split-track begins at point 70. (See page 3)

BRENTWOOD
—M U S I C—

Copyright © MCMXCIV New Spring Publishing/ASCAP, a division of Brentwood Music, Inc.,
One Maryland Farms, Suite 200, Brentwood, TN 37027. All rights reserved. Unauthorized duplication prohibited.
DISTRIBUTED BY BRENTWOOD MUSIC.

Christmas, Sing Noel!

Words by
WILLIAM DODD

Music by
ED KEE

1. Join in the cel - e - bra - tion— sing
2. O what a gift___ from heav - en, such

4

5

NARRATOR:

Christmas… that most wonderful time of the year when all the world rejoices! *(music begins)* Singing, laughter and joy are a part of the celebration that fills every home. Some celebrate the <u>season</u>… others celebrate a feeling of peace and goodwill… while many look to friends and family as the focal point of <u>their</u> celebrations. But how **blessed** are those who celebrate the One whose coming brings everlasting joy… the One whose coming brought mankind the greatest reason for joy that the world has ever known! That One was Jesus– God in human flesh, who came to earth to dwell with men and redeem them to Himself. *(underscore ends – pause tape)*

This is the greatest news one can hear. It makes the heart want to sing for joy. It's such a simple story– *(song intro begins)* yet so marvelous that we love to sing its message over and over again. Christmas is a time for singing… for Christ has come. The King is born!

Underscore One

("Sing We Now of Christmas")

Arranged by Ed Kee

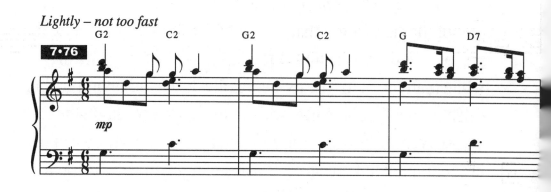

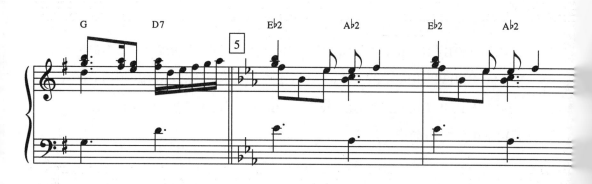

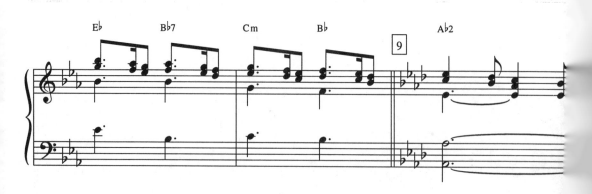

Segue to "Sing We Now of Christmas".

Sing We Now of Christmas

Original Lyrics by
ED KEE

Traditional Polish Carol

18

20

NARRATOR:

Long before the world began, God planned His glorious means of redemption for mankind. *(music begins)* From the very beginning, the mystery and wonder surrounding this miraculous event has inspired the human heart to spontaneous songs of praise. Mary, overwhelmed that God would choose her to bear His Son, sang her praise back to Him when she said, "My soul glorifies the Lord and my spirit rejoices in God, my Savior."

Though she was overjoyed at all that God had told her she still must have had many unanswered questions… for it was all so mysterious… too wonderful to comprehend! Yet her confidence in God never faltered. Mary understood that every question earth cannot answer… heaven knows.

Underscore Two

("Heaven Knows")

Arranged by Ed Kee

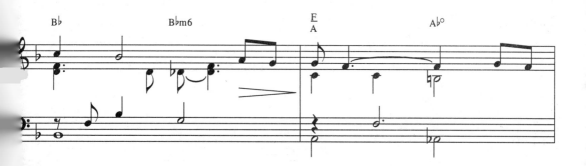

Segue to: "Heaven Knows".

Heaven Knows

Words by
WILLIAM DODD and ED KEE

Music by
ED KEE

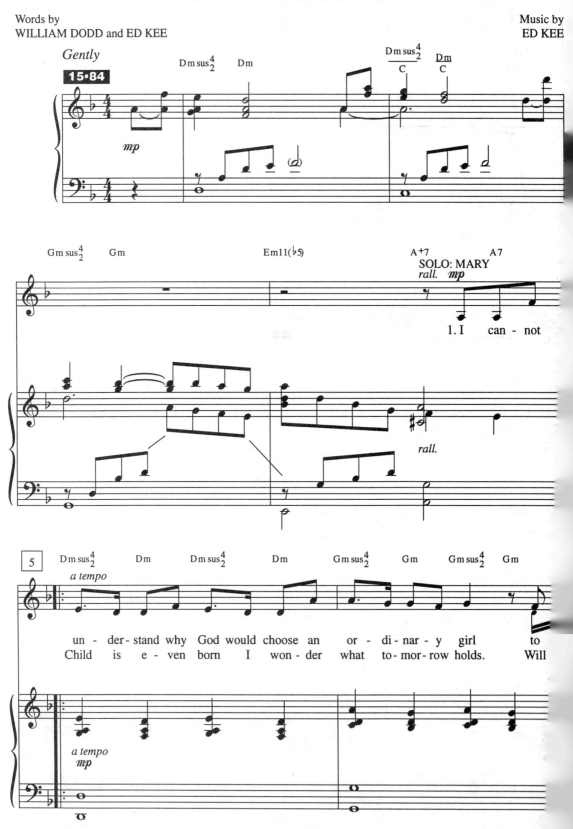

17•86

18•87

32

NARRATOR:

God was not to let His arrival here on earth go unannounced. Yet it was not to the rich and noble that He came to announce the Savior's birth… *(music begins)* but He chose a band of lowly shepherds who were out in the fields at night keeping watch over their flocks. An angel of the Lord appeared to them, and the glory of the Lord shone all around them… and they were terrified! But their fear soon turned to amazement and joy… for as the angel finished telling them the "good news" of Jesus' birth, the whole night sky was suddenly filled with angels… singing God's praises with a heavenly "noel"!

Underscore Three

("Good News of Great Joy")

Arranged by Ed Kee

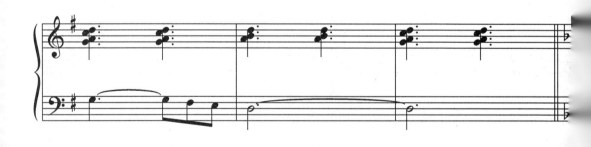

Segue to "Good News of Grea...

Good News of Great Joy

Words by
WILLIAM DODD

Music by
ED KEE

Out on the hill-side the shep-herds were faith-ful-ly
Heav-en's an-nounce-ment went out to the low-ly who

36

watch - ing their flocks in the night-- When an
sought not for glo - ry or fame; Still they

an - gel ap - peared in a vi - sion of glo - ry and
left all they had on the hill - side be - hind when the

21•90 *1st time*
24•93 *2nd time*

they were a - fraid at the sight. But
call un - to Beth - le - hem came. They

40

41

Speak the Name of Jesus

(Joseph, Mary)

Words by
WILLIAM DODD and ED KEE

Music by
ED KEE

With much expression

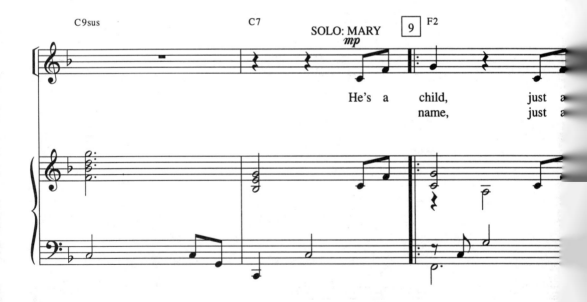

29•98 *2nd time*

NARRATOR:

(Underscored) If the morning stars sang together when God set the cornerstone of the world in its place, then surely the stars must have sung at the birth of the Lord Jesus. There were many stars in the heavens on the night of Jesus' birth– but there was <u>one</u> whose song stood out above the rest. Its majestic voice reached to the <u>far</u> corners of the earth to summon wise men from the east… great rulers who <u>knew</u> of such things as stars… and kings. Its brilliant light called them to worship in Bethlehem.

The Heavens Are Telling

Words by
WILLIAM DODD and ED KEE

Music by
ED KEE

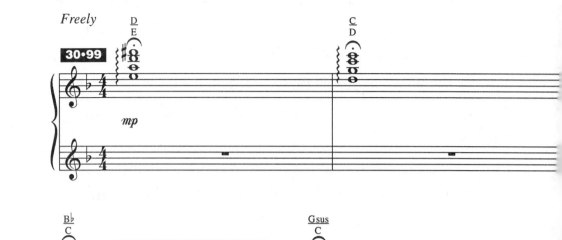

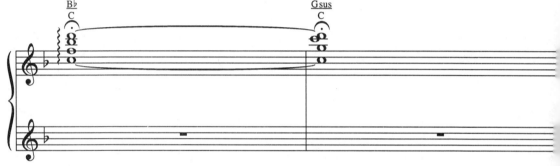

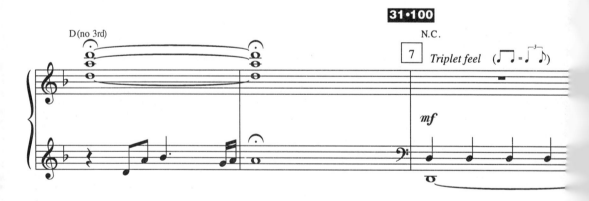

CHOIR - *(1st time only)*
MALE SOLO - *(2nd time only)*

1. Wise men watched the stars by night, search - ing for a
2. Days we've trav - eled o - ver land— tired and wea - ry,

mp - (March-like)

sign in the heav - ens; There they saw a
still we are seek - ing Through the des - ert's

glor - ious light call - ing from a -
burn - ing sand to find the Ho - ly

yearn - ing   to find Him and wor - ship   with gifts we

33•102

(Repeat to bar 11.)

bring.   bring.

1.   (Repeat to bar 11.)   2.

1.   (Repeat to bar 11.)   2.

•104

mf

54

King_____ of Is - ra - el.   The heav - ens are

tell - ing_____ a mar- vel- ous sto - ry—   for God in His

glo — ry   has giv- en a new - born King!   The star bright-ly

58

NARRATOR:

(Underscored) Many songs were sung that first Christmas by those whom God chose to play a special part in His coming. One whose prophetic song still speaks to the nations of the earth was Simeon. He saw the Christ Child with his own eyes; yet, through the eyes of faith, he saw not only **his** salvation, but the salvation of all those who would believe on Him. For, as he gently took the Baby in his arms, he said, "**He** is the Light that will shine upon the nations, and **He** will be the glory of your people, Israel."

Underscore Four

("A Light to the Nations")

Moderately

Arranged by Ed Kee

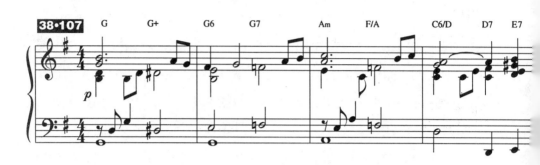

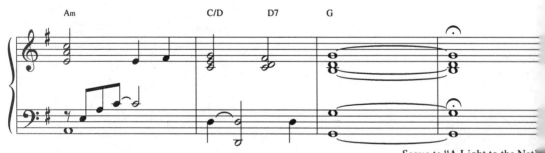

Segue to "A Light to the Nati

A Light to the Nations

Words by
WILLIAM DODD

Music by
ED KEE

62

na-tions, a ref-uge of hope_____ for all men,_____

Wait-ing with arms wide o-pen, no mat-ter how

dark the long night has been._____ Re-demp-tion He of-fers

INVITATION (optional)

(to be given by Pastor or Narrator)

Today we celebrate the coming of Jesus. He was God in human flesh who came to earth so that we could <u>know</u> Him. Unfortunately, the only thing that many people ever know of Jesus is what they hear at Christmas… that He was a baby born in a manger. Yet, there is so much more.

For those who truly know Him, Christmas is a time of real joy. The song you have just heard gives the reason. You see, before Jesus came, **there was no light**. The scripture describes our condition as "people walking in darkness…living in the land of the shadow of death." (ISAIAH 9:2) But it goes on to say that "the people that walked in darkness have seen a great light. They that dwell in the land of the shadow of death, upon <u>them</u> the light has shined." <u>Jesus</u> is that light. He allows us to see ourselves as we really are. He has come for all men– everywhere. He comes bringing hope and light to those who are groping to find their way in this dark world.

Many people blindly stumble through life in spiritual darkness– confused, fearful, uncertain about where they are going. Does that describe your life right now? If so, God can penetrate the very depths of your soul with His light, and turn your darkness into the brightest day. That's the reason He came. He gave Himself to save you from <u>eternal</u> darkness and separation from God. He wants you to know Him and to live forever in His everlasting light.

He came into a world darkened by sin and was born in a lowly cattle stall. His mother placed Him in a dirty manger. No one cleaned the stable before Jesus came, yet it was there that He chose to be born. Today, He wants to be born in your heart. There is no need to "clean up" before He comes. All He asks is that you humble your heart and invite Him into your life. Won't you do that today right where you are?

PRAYER *(optional)*

Make Your Heart a Bethlehem

Words by
WILLIAM DODD

Music by
ED KEE

70

faith - ful few would wel - come Him in - stead._____
still be less that Christ is wor - thy of._____

_____ And the cit - y was so crowd - ed that
_____ All He wants that real - ly mat - ters is

man - y nev - er knew; But just as He was
just an o - pen door Where He can come and

* Lyric changes from "To" to "So" 2nd time only.

74

and find a place that He can use— He's wait - ing now for

50•119 *2nd time*

you to ask Him in,_____ For on - ly

He can make your heart a Beth - le - hem.

NARRATOR:

"Sing for joy, O heavens, for the Lord has done this; *(music begins)* shout aloud, O earth beneath. Burst into song, you mountains, you forests and all your trees, for the Lord has redeemed Jacob, He displays His glory in Israel."*

(Segue without pause to "Celebrate the King.*")*

*(Isaiah 44:23 NIV

Redeemed to Praise

Words by
WILLIAM DODD

Music by
ED KEE

With energy!

SA - *(Both times)* **mf**
Add TB - *(2nd time only)* **mf**

When the heart that You_____ cre -
think a - bout_____ re -

80

praise, The Sav - ior longs to hear___ from those re - deemed to praise.___

Segue without pause to "Celebrate the

Celebrate the King

(Carol Medley)

Arranged by Ed Kee

Forcefully ("bell-like")

"Joy to the World!" (ISAAC WATTS, G. F. HANDEL)

CHOIR* - *f*

Joy to the world! the Lord is come! Let

earth re - ceive her

:egation may join choir.

86

58·127

"For Unto Us a Child Is Born" (G. F. HANDEL)

King!

For un-to us a Child is born—— un-to us a Son is

giv- en, un- to us a Son is

Prince of Peace– The Ev-er-last-ing Fa-ther, the

Prince of Peace!

"Hark! The Herald Angels Sing" (CHARLES WESLEY, FELIX MENDELSSOHN)

Joy-ful, all ye na-tions rise,___ join the tri - umph

89

"Angels We Have Heard on High" (French Carol)

"O Come, All Ye Faithful" (JOHN FRANCIS WADE)

come, let us a - dore Him, O come, let us a -

dore Him, O come,_ let us a - dore_ Him:_

92

"O Holy Night" (JOHN S. DWIGHT, ADOLPHE C. ADAM)

Christ the Lord!

Fall on your knees— O

Christmas, Sing Noel!
Reprise

Words by
WILLIAM DODD

Music by
ED KEE

Join in the cel - e - bra - tion— sing
O what a gift from heav - en, such

prais - es, ev - 'ry - one!_____
won - drous love____ dis - played!_____

'Tis the sea - son to re - joice for
Is it an - y won - der why we

Christ the Lord___ has come:_____
cel - e - brate___ this way?_____

98

2.
F

Bb/F   F

el!

45 Asus   A   Dm   C/E   F
mp

Let us lift___ our   prais - es   for   the   Lord   to hear,_____

mp

(ALL)   Dsus   D7   Gm   Gm/F

_____   And   cel - e - brate___ this   glor - ious   time   of

CHRISTMAS, SING NOEL!
Dramatic Production
Script

Song #1: "Christmas, Sing Noel!"

NARRATION #1

Christmas ! That most wonderful time of year when all the world rejoices ! *(music begins)* Singing and laughter and joy are a part of the celebration that fills every home. Some celebrate the season… others celebrate a feeling of peace and goodwill… while many look to friends and family as the focal point of their celebrations. But how blessed are those who celebrate the One whose coming brings everlasting joy. The One whose coming brought mankind the greatest reason for joy that the world has ever known ! That One was Jesus — God in human flesh, who came to earth to dwell with men and redeem them to Himself. *(underscore ends – pause tape)*

This is the greatest news one can hear. It makes the heart want to sing for joy. It's such a simple story, *(song intro begins)* yet so marvelous that we love to sing its message over and over again. Christmas is a time for singing… for Christ has come… the King is born !

Song #2: "Sing We Now of Christmas"

NARRATION #2 and MARY MONOLOGUE

(by Grace Marestaing)   (approx. time 2:30)

NARRATOR:
Long before the world began, God planned His glorious means of redemption for mankind. From the very beginning the mystery and wonder surrounding this miraculous event has inspired the human heart to spontaneous song. It inspired a very personal song of praise from a young woman named Mary.

MARY:
I am just an ordinary girl — I have to keep reminding myself — just an ordinary girl. I am… really. I'm not sure, but part of me feels like I've won a prize for which I've not competed, and part of me feels awed and… afraid.

My life was simple… I'm engaged… I'm engaged to Joseph, the carpenter. He's been so kind, so loving. He's as much in awe as I am.

Just think of it — angels don't make appointments, you know. All of a sudden there he was, the light filling the room… telling me I was highly favored. I just stood there shaking till he said, "Mary, you have nothing to fear, God has a surprise for you…"

A surprise… Messiah… I am carrying the promised One of Israel!

(underscore begins) I had to share my news with someone who would understand — that was Elizabeth. Since that day with Elizabeth I just can't help repeating that my soul glorifies the Lord. What God has done for me will never be forgotten… I just can't seem to take it all in. Dear Lord… I'm just a girl . Only You know what's ahead.

NARRATOR:
(song intro begins) It was all so mysterious… too wonderful to comprehend. Yet, her confidence in God never faltered. Mary understood that every question earth cannot answer… heaven knows.

Song #3: "Heaven Knows"

NARRATION #3

God was not to let his arrival here on earth go unannounced. Yet it was not to the rich and noble that He came *(underscore begins)* to announce the Savior's birth… but He chose a band of lowly shepherds who were out in the fields at night, keeping watch over their flocks. An angel of the Lord appeared to them and the glory of the Lord shone all around them… and they were terrified. But their fear soon turned to amazement and joy… for as the angel finished telling them the "good news" of Jesus's birth, *(song intro begins)* the whole night sky was suddenly filled with angels… singing God's praises with a heavenly Noel !

Song #4: "Good News of Great Joy"

NARRATION #4 and MARY & JOSEPH DIALOGUE

(by Grace Marestaing)   (approx. time 2:10)

NARRATOR:
God knew what He was doing from the very beginning. He intimately knew the lives and faith of the Jewish girl and the carpenter. He knew the challenges and the privilege that would follow for the young parents of His Son. And the beginning had been a mixture of the harsh realities and doubts along with a sense of awe at all that had happened.

After the flurry of activity Mary and Joseph settled into a reflective quiet. Joseph, exhausted and silent is almost mesmerized as he stares in wonder at the Child.

MARY:
Joseph… you can touch him. It's… alright.

JOSEPH:
(KEEPS STARING THEN HESITANTLY REACHES TO TOUCH THE BABY) How tiny his hand is… I don't know, Mary — some things are… they're… (SIGHS)

MARY:
I know… almost too much to understand.

JOSEPH:
I'll never forget the angel…

MARY:

… and the dream.

JOSEPH:

"Joseph, son of David, don't be afraid… don't be afraid to make Mary your wife. The child she's carrying is conceived of God's Holy Spirit." Mary just look at his tiny hand, these tiny feet… Here He is.

MARY:

Emmanuel — God is with us… God is with us, Joseph.

JOSEPH:

I remember the word of the angel distinctly *(intro to song begins)* — "you, Joseph will name Him." Mary, I'm to name Him… "You will name Him Jesus…"

Song #5: Speak the Name of Jesus

NARRATION #5

(Underscored) If the morning stars sang together when God set the cornerstone of the world in its place, then surely the stars must have sung at the birth of the Lord Jesus. There were many stars in the heavens on the night of Jesus' birth — but there was one whose song stood out above the rest. Its majestic voice reached great rulers who knew of such things as stars… and kings. It's brilliant light called them to worship in Bethlehem.

Song #6: "The Heavens Are Telling"

NARRATION #6 and SIMEON MONOLOGUE

(by Grace Marestaing)   (approx. time 3:10)

Many songs were sung that first Christmas by those whom God chose to play a special part in His coming. One whose prophetic song still speaks to the nations of the earth was Simeon. He had lived his life in prayerful expectancy of help for Israel.

SIMEON:

You cannot begin to imagine the thoughts and feelings that went through this old man that day. They had to do with a promise, simply a promise — and God's promise at that.

You see, Yahweh,… the faith, prayer has always been, well… important to me. I was well acquainted with the Scriptures — the prophecies that spoke of Messiah and the promised help for Israel. I can't tell you exactly when or how, but I do know that somewhere along the line the promise became very personal. I was deeply impressed that the time was closer at hand then any of us ever imagined. Through God's Spirit, I became convinced that I would actually see Messiah before I died.

I didn't necessarily go around telling everyone,… as a matter of fact even though the promise remained imprinted deep within me, many times the routines and pressures of life made me question if I had heard right. To tell you the truth, that's kind of where I was on that day…

It was my practice to go to Temple daily and that's where I was headed... but that day the Spirit caught my attention and something... something unusual, out of my ordinary routine, was drawing me there. *(underscore begins)* As I walked into the temple courts, I noticed the young couple with the baby boy. It was as if Yahweh himself was tapping me on the shoulder, sheepishly grinning and saying, "Excuse me, remember the promise?" I couldn't help myself... I... I had to touch... to hold this child and, amazingly enough his mother was willing. Everything just welled up inside me... It was as if I was given new vision and could see, and new ears to hear... my understanding opened. There He was — the Promise made flesh.

O Sovereign Lord, You can release me in peace as You promised. I've now seen Your salvation with my own eyes; it's out in the open for everyone to see: *(intro to song begins)* This is the God-revealing light that will shine upon the nations, and the glory of Your people, Israel .

Song #7: "A Light to the Nations"

NARRATION #7 — Pastoral Response and Invitation
Feel free to handle this in a way that is appropriate to your church custom and setting. (A suggested format may be found on page 68.)

Song #8: "Make Your Heart a Bethlehem"

NARRATION #8
"Sing for joy, O heavens, for the Lord has done this; *(intro to song begins)* shout aloud, O earth beneath. Burst into song, you mountains, you forests and all your trees, for the Lord has redeemed Jacob, He displays His glory in Israel." (Is. 44:23)

Song #9: "Redeemed to Praise"

Song #10: "Celebrate the King" – Carol Medley

Song #11: "Christmas, Sing Noel!" – Reprise

CHRISTMAS, SING NOEL!

Production and Staging Ideas
by Jacquelyn Coffey

To the music director:

CHRISTMAS, SING NOEL! can be effectively produced in concert using a choir, soloists and narrator, or elaborately produced using dramatic characterization, sets, costumes and many cast members. The purpose of these notes is to spark your creativity as you think of the resources available in your church setting. Let them be a starting point as you and your choir prepare this musical gift for your congregation.

PARTICIPANTS:

SPEAKING	SINGING	NON-SPEAKING
Narrator	Choir	Angel Movement Choir *(optional)*
Mary *(optional)*	Mary	Shepherds
Joseph *(optional)*	Joseph	Prophets
Simeon *(optional)*	Wise Men *(optional)*	Wise Men's entourage *(optional)*

STAGE SETTING

The staging area is divided into four parts:

1. *A CHOIR AREA UPSTAGE CENTER.* Behind the choir is a painted backdrop of the Bethlehem night sky.

2. *THE AREA DOWNSTAGE CENTER FROM THE CHOIR.* This area is used for Mary's solo, Simeon's scene and the arrival of the Shepherds and the Wise Men to the manger.

3. *THE SHEPHERD'S HILLSIDE AREA STAGE RIGHT.* This area is defined by a painted backdrop of a hillside and night sky. Upstage of this area is an elevated platform for the Angels to appear to the Shepherds. The Wise Men will also use this area as they look for their way to Bethlehem.

4. *THE MANGER AREA STAGE LEFT.* This area is defined by a painted backdrop of the manger stall with Bethlehem in the background. Above the backdrop hangs the Bethlehem star. Upstage of this area is an elevated platform for the Angels to appear at the manger.

The Narrator is positioned DOWNSTAGE RIGHT between the shepherd's hillside area and the choir.

LIGHTING

The lights should be able to cross-fade between the four general playing areas and the Narrator. Light intensity and color changes for each area. This will help create the mood and focus for the scenes. During the slide presentation for "The Heavens Are Telling," softly light the choir without washing out the slide projections. Specialty lighting requirements would include: STAGE RIGHT for the appearance of the Angels to the Shepherds, intensity control of the Bethlehem star, and a special light radiating from the baby Jesus for the finale.

SLIDE SHOW OR MULTI MEDIA

Slide presentations would be effective during the songs "Sing We Now of Christmas" and "The Heavens Are Telling."

During "Sing We Now of Christmas," project appropriate slides of the Christmas story as the choir sings. Ready-made slide sets are available from several producers. The names and sources may be obtained from your Christian book seller, or you may create your own slide show by photographing the art work of the great masters. There are many beautiful art books at most libraries, or check with your local museum or university. (Check first for copyright approval!)

During the narrative that precedes "The Heavens Are Telling," project slides of the galaxies and stars. These slides can be obtained in sets by writing or visiting an observatory. Again, a library or a nearby university may be able to supply additional sources of photographs or the address of an observatory in your area.

If you decide to use slides, the projection screen would be most effectively placed above the backdrop that is behind the choir. This will make the projected stars look like an extension of the night sky.

MOVEMENT AND CHOREOGRAPHY

If you have people with talent in choreography and movement, there are several sections that would benefit. An Angel Movement Choir can interpret the announcement to the Shepherds. They can also dance the chorus during "Good News of Great Joy," and during the "Gloria" section of "Celebrate the King" – the carol medley. The singing choir can do simple hand movements of praise during the song "Redeemed to Praise."

The purpose of choreography is to capture the mood and style of the music and to make the lyrics visible. Don't be afraid of simple movement. Done well, they can be very effective. (Don't overdo choreography or feel that every piece needs to have movement. Standing still can be an effective visual rest and point of contrast for your audience and your performers.)

COSTUMES

The choir may be in festive Christmas attire or choir robes. The Narrator also may be in contemporary clothes as appropriate for your audience. The characters depicting the story should all dress in biblical costumes.

STAGING AND BLOCKING

STAGE LANGUAGE:

BLOCK: to pattern the physical movement or traffic between actors on stage

CROSS: to walk from one stage position to another

STAY OPEN or OPEN UP: when delivering lines the actor's face and body stay visible to the audience: When two actors are dialoguing both need to "stay open" to the audience.

EXIT: to leave the stage area

DOWNSTAGE: the part of the stage closest to the audience

UPSTAGE: the part of the stage farthest from the audience

STAGE RIGHT: the performer's right as he/she faces the audience

STAGE LEFT: the performer's left as he/she faces the audience

BASIC BLOCKING:

The purpose of blocking is to give sense to the words and actions of the actors and singers. The blocking also helps the audience to see what is important and ignore what is unimportant. An audience 'reads' a stage as they read a book; they look at the stage from their left to their right. This is a natural visual flow. When blocking, use this natural flow to your advantage by starting scenes on STAGE RIGHT (which is the audience's left), and travel the dialogue or movement to STAGE LEFT (which is the audience's right). Position the most important dialogue CENTER STAGE. This might sound complicated, but once you start working with this concept it will help the blocking make "visual" sense to the audience.

Song #1: "Christmas, Sing Noel!"

The stage begins in black. The choir is in position CENTER STAGE. During the introduction the lights come up on the choir and the DOWNSTAGE area. As the choir sings, groups of friends and families enter the stage area from every direction. They carry presents, greet one another and exchange gifts. The scene is a warm family atmosphere of the activities of Christmas.

"Underscore One"

The lights hold on the choir and DOWNSTAGE activity area and come up on the Narrator STAGE RIGHT. As the Narrator speaks, the DOWNSTAGE activity continues with family and friends gathering, exchanging gifts and gathering around a Christmas dinner table.

Song #2: "Sing We Now of Christmas"

The light slowly fades out on Narrator and choir as the slide projection of artwork begins.

VERSE 1: The baby Jesus in the manger as Mary, Joseph and the Angels look on.

VERSE 2: The Angel's announcement to the Shepherds and the Shepherd's arrival at the manger.

VERSE 3: The Wise Men on their journey following the star and their arrival at the manger.

VERSE 4: The Wise Men bowing down and presenting gifts before the baby Jesus (End the song with a slide that shows the entire manger scene, including Jesus, Mary and Joseph, the Angels, Shepherds and Wise Men.)

"Underscore Two" (and/or *optional* Mary monologue)

Lights go out on the projectors and come up on the Narrator. Mary enters from STAGE RIGHT and crosses to CENTER STAGE. The lights slowly come up on Mary. As the Narrator finishes, his light slowly goes out. Mary delivers her monologue or sings from this CENTER STAGE position.

Song #3: "Heaven Knows"

Mary sings. The lights come up on the choir as they sing.

"Underscore Three"

The lights cross-fade, going out on Mary and the choir, and coming up on the Narrator. Mary exits. As the Narrator describes the announcement by the Angels to the Shepherds, a light suddenly appears on the hillside STAGE RIGHT. The Angels pantomime the announcement to the Shepherds as the Narrator speaks. The Shepherds watch and listen to the Angels in amazement. The Bethlehem star begins to glow over the manger area STAGE LEFT. The lights on STAGE LEFT come up. Mary and Joseph are kneeling at the manger, looking at the newborn baby Jesus.

Song #4: "Good News of Great Joy"

The light remains on the Shepherds and the Angels and goes out on the Narrator. The lights come up on the choir as the choir sings. Block the Shepherds to describe the words that are being sung by the choir. The Angel Choir can pantomime the first verse and then dance to each repeat of the chorus on their elevated platform.

VERSE 1: The Shepherds are watching as the Angels appear.
EVERY CHORUS: The Angels interpret the words of the song with movements.
VERSE 2: The Shepherds leave the hillside and travel to the manger.

The song ends with the Shepherds kneeling before the manger as Mary and Joseph look on.

Optional narration with Mary & Joseph dialogue

The lights slowly come back up on the Narrator. The Shepherds exit the manger area. As the Narrator finishes, his light slowly goes out. Mary and Joseph remain STAGE LEFT, alone with the baby Jesus. They deliver their dialogue and sing from this position.

Song #5: "Speak the Name of Jesus"

Mary and Joseph sing their duet from STAGE LEFT. They kneel at the manger. During the song, Mary picks up the baby and stands. Mary hands the baby to Joseph. Joseph sings.

Narration with underscore

The light remains at the manger scene. Mary and Joseph return the baby Jesus to the manger. They kneel by His side. The lights slowly go up on the Narrator STAGE RIGHT. As the Narrator speaks, slides of the heavens, stars, moons and galaxies are projected.

Song #6: "The Heavens Are Telling"

The light goes out on the Narrator and comes up on the choir CENTER STAGE and the Wise Men in the hills STAGE RIGHT. The Wise Men look up at the star of Bethlehem STAGE LEFT. Block the Wise Men to describe the words being sung by the choir. During each chorus continue to project the slides of the stars and galaxies. Hold the projector on one slide during the verses.

> VERSE 1: The Wise Men are STAGE RIGHT in the hillside, watching the stars.
> VERSE 2: The Wise Men travel toward the manger. The soloist sings as they travel.
> VERSE 3: The Wise Men meet the Prophets CENTER STAGE, the Prophets point the way to Bethlehem.
> VERSE 4: The Wise Men arrive at the manger.
> VERSE 5: The Wise Men present their gifts to the baby Jesus. They kneel at the manger. Mary and Joseph look on in wonder.

"Underscore Four" (or *optional* narration with Simeon monologue)

The light slowly comes up on Narrator STAGE RIGHT. The Wise Men exit. Mary and Joseph, carrying the baby Jesus leave the manger and cross to CENTER STAGE. On the way to the temple they meet Simeon. Mary hands the baby to Simeon. Simeon is overjoyed. He hands the baby back to Mary and Joseph. Mary and Joseph exit. (If you are doing the optional monologue, Simeon would speak after Mary and Joseph exit. If you are not, then go directly into the song.) The lights slowly go out on the Narrator and Simeon and come up on the choir.

Song #7: "A Light to the Nations"

The lights come up on the choir and the choir sings.

Pastoral Response and Invitation

Feel free to handle this in a way that is appropriate to your church custom and setting.

Song #8: "Make Your Heart a Bethlehem"

The lights come up on the choir and the choir sings.

Narration

The light comes up on the Narrator and the Narrator speaks.